BIBLE STORY SEARCH

written by Tracy Harrast
illustrated by Steve Cox

CONCORDIA PUBLISHING HOUSE • SAINT LOUIS

Can you find:

3 butterflies

2 colorful parrots

6 fireflies

2 dragonflies

1 pinecone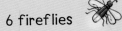

4 bananas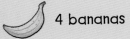

1 worm

5 yellow flowers

2 squirrels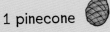

1 ladybug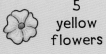

1 monkey

1 frog

1 green apple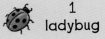

1 hummingbird

God Creates a Wonderful World

When God made the world, He did it in six days. At first there was only darkness, but then God said, "Let there be light!" and there was light! That was the first day. On the second day, He separated the water from the air and made the blue sky. The third day was when He separated land from seas and made plants and trees. On the fourth day, God created the sun, moon, and sparkling stars. On the fifth day, He filled the sea with fish and the sky with birds. On the sixth day, He created land animals and people.

God formed the first man out of the dust. He breathed life into him, named him Adam, and put him in the Garden of Eden to take care of it. God said it wasn't good for Adam to be alone. He took one of Adam's ribs and made a woman, Eve, who would be Adam's wife. God said that everything He made was good.

Can you find:

- 2 snails
- 2 rats
- 2 pigs
- 2 spiders
- 2 flamingoes
- 2 snakes
- 2 turtles
- 2 skunks
- 2 hedgehogs
- 2 koalas
- 2 fish
- 2 jellyfish
- 2 doves
- 2 bats
- 2 rabbits

God Saves Noah and the Animals

The world was good when God first made it, but Adam and Eve sinned and could no longer live in the Garden of Eden. Their children, grandchildren and all people kept sinning and this made God very sad. The world became completely evil except for just one man—Noah!

God planned to flood the whole world to make it clean again. He told Noah to build a boat, where it would be safe for Noah, his family, and a pair of every kind of animal. Noah obeyed, and when the ark was ready, God sent the animals.

Rain fell for forty days and forty nights until the whole world was covered in water. Finally the rain stopped. After many months, the floodwaters dried up enough that Noah's family and the animals could leave the ark. They built an altar and prayed to God. Then God stretched a rainbow across the sky as a reminder of His promise to never flood the earth again.

Can you find:

1 grasshopper

2 chariots

3 camels

4 satchels

1 donkey with pack

4 stone blocks

1 gold cup

4 sheep

4 blue butterflies

this symbol

this symbol

3 horses

2 cats

1 lotus flower

God Brings Good from Evil

Joseph's twelve brothers were jealous because their dad gave him a fancy coat. Joseph was his favorite son. One day, Joseph told them he dreamed they would bow to him. The brothers were very angry, so they sold him to some travelers. Joseph became a slave in Egypt.

A few years later, a woman lied about him and had him sent to prison. In jail, Joseph told people the meanings of their dreams, and one of them told Pharaoh about this gift. So Pharaoh asked Joseph to come tell him the meanings of his dreams. Joseph did, so Pharoah let him out of jail, and gave him an important job. In time, Joseph became the second most powerful man in Egypt! Pharaoh put Joseph in charge of storing food so people would not starve during the famine—a time when the crops would not grow.

Joseph's brothers came to Egypt and asked him for food. It had been many years, and they didn't recognize him. But Joseph knew who they were, and he forgave them. He said, "You meant to harm me, but God used it for good to save many lives!"

Can you find:

3 scorpions

1 harp

1 flag

1 yellow headband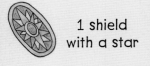

1 striped tent

1 shield with a star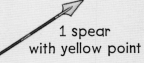

1 shield with an X

1 spear with yellow point

this armour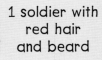

1 soldier with red hair and beard

5 smooth stones

3 lizards

1 helmet with green feather

God Helps the Little Guy

Goliath was a giant Philistine soldier. He told the Israelite army, "Send whoever you want to fight me. If he kills me, your army wins. If I kill him, my army wins." The Israelite soldiers were all too scared to fight Goliath. But a young shepherd named David was there with his big brothers. God filled David with courage.

David said, "The Lord saved me from the lion and the bear and I know He will save me from Goliath, too!"

David gathered five smooth stones. When Goliath teased him, David answered, "You come against me with sword, spear, and javelin. But I come against you in the name of the Lord Almighty!" Then David sent a stone flying out of his sling. It hit the giant's forehead and killed him. With God on his side, David had won with just a sling and a stone!

Can you find:

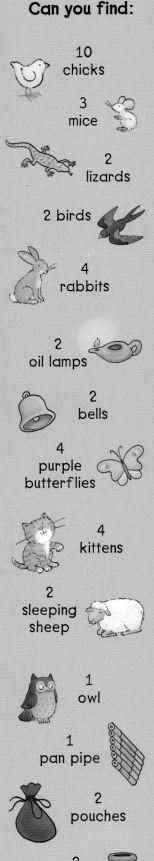

10
chicks

3
mice

2
lizards

2 birds

4
rabbits

2
oil lamps

2
bells

4
purple
butterflies

4
kittens

2
sleeping
sheep

1
owl

1
pan pipe

2
pouches

2
urns

1
trumpet

God with Us

God sent the angel Gabriel to a young woman named Mary. Gabriel told her she would give birth to the Son of God. She answered, "I am the Lord's servant. May it happen to me as you say." She was planning to marry Joseph.

In a dream, Gabriel told Joseph, "Name the baby Jesus, because He will save His people from their sins."

Months after Mary and Joseph married, they were on a trip to Bethlehem when it was time for God's Son to be born. There was no room in the inn, so they stayed in a stable. And that's where Jesus was born! In nearby fields, an angel appeared to shepherds and said, "Your Savior has been born! He is Christ, the Lord. You will find Him wrapped in cloths, lying in a manger." The shepherds went to find Jesus and worshiped him.

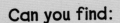

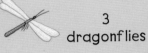
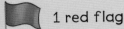

Jesus Chooses Twelve Helpers

Jesus chose twelve helpers called disciples. He didn't pick men who were famous, rich, popular, or even educated. He chose ordinary people who were willing to give up everything to follow Him. Four were fishermen—brothers Andrew and Simon Peter and two other brothers named James and John. One disciple was a tax collector named Matthew. Another was a twin named Thomas. John the Baptist's disciple Philip and Philip's friend Nathaniel became Jesus' disciples, too.

Jesus chose two disciples named Judas—one was faithful, but the other was not. One disciple was called Simon the Zealot, and another was James the son of Alphaeus.

When Jesus said to some of these men, "Come follow Me," they quit whatever they were doing and followed Him. They learned from Him, performed miracles in His name, and led many to believe in Him.

Can you find:

1
dog

2
Roman
soldiers

1
striped hat

7 ants

1
man holding
a cat

1 woman with
water jug

2
lizards

3
birds

1
cricket

2
men with
turbans

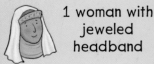
1 woman with
jeweled
headband

1
fish with
purple tail

1 man with
red striped
cloak

1 donkey

Jesus Feeds More Than 5,000

One day, Jesus and His disciples took a boat ride to another place. A large crowd of people found them anyway! Jesus taught the crowd and healed their illnesses. Then His disciples said, "It is getting late. Send these people away so they can get a meal somewhere."

Jesus said, "They do not need to go away. You give them something to eat." Jesus asked how much food they already had.

"We only have five loaves of bread and two fish. It is not enough for everyone," they replied.

Jesus prayed to thank God for the food. Next He broke the bread into pieces. He gave pieces of bread and fish to the disciples, and they gave them to the people. More than five thousand people ate all that they wanted, and there were still twelve basketfuls of leftovers. It was a miracle!

Can you find:

1 doll

1 striped water jug

3 pigeons

1 hat with feather

1 apple

2 gourds

6 bees

2 cats

1 cobra

1 cup

3 Roman soldiers

8 gold coins

3 rats

Jesus Rides Like a King

In Bible times, kings sometimes entered cities riding donkeys. Long before Jesus was born, a prophet had said about Israel's future king: "See, your king comes to you, righteous and having salvation, gentle and riding on a donkey."

One day Jesus told his disciples where they could find a donkey for Him to ride. He told them that if anyone asked why they were untying it, they should say, "The Lord needs it and will send it back

soon," and the person would let them have the donkey.

That's exactly what happened. When Jesus entered Jerusalem riding on a donkey like a king, the people waved palm branches and shouted, "Hosanna!" which means "Save us!" They also called, "Blessed is the king who comes in the name of the Lord!"

The church leaders told Jesus to scold His followers for being noisy. He said, "If they keep quiet, the stones will cry out!"

Can you find:

1 rooster

5 sandals

1 carrot

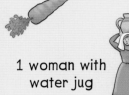
1 woman with water jug

3 flies

3 cats

1 donkey

1 goblet

1 ring

2 mice

6 eggs

1 sleeping boy

2 oil lamps

4 olives

1 goat

Jesus' Last Supper

Jesus had come to give His life on a cross so that whoever believed in Him would be forgiven and live with Him in heaven. The night before Jesus died, He ate His last supper with His disciples. It was an important festival called Passover.

During that meal, Jesus told the disciples many important things. He said, "As I have loved you, love one another. By this people will know you are My disciples: if you have love for one another."

He gave them bread and said it was His body for them. Then He gave them a cup and said it was His blood poured out for forgiveness of sins. He comforted them by telling them about heaven, "In My Father's house are many rooms. I am going to prepare a place for you. I will come back and take you to be with Me."

Look Again!
Can you find all these things inside the book?
Use your magnifying glass to help you!

 a campfire

 a baby

a big star

5 pears

 a leaping lamb

 2 stoneworkers

 2 scallop shells

a red sea star

 a monkey with a banana

 2 blue birds

a soldier with
a white beard

a bunch of grapes

8 figs

 a waving fisherman

 a woman in
an orange cloak

 a shepherd holding a lamb

For more fun, look for this
symbol hidden in every scene.